This book belongs to:

....

This exciting and fun Book "I Spy Everything" a is guessing game picture for Kids Ages 2-5 . It presents A B C activities for Kids with fun and interactive pictures

May your kids 'days be full of endless joy and happiness.

If you enjoy the book, please leave us a review wherever you bought it.

BY: CLARA FINLORD

Enjoy!

I SPY with my smart eye, Something beginning with...

A IS FOR

ALBATROSS

I SPY with my smart eye, Something beginning with...

 **IS FOR**

BANANA

I SPY with my smart eye, Something beginning with...

C IS FOR

CUPCAKE

I SPY with my smart eye, Something beginning with...

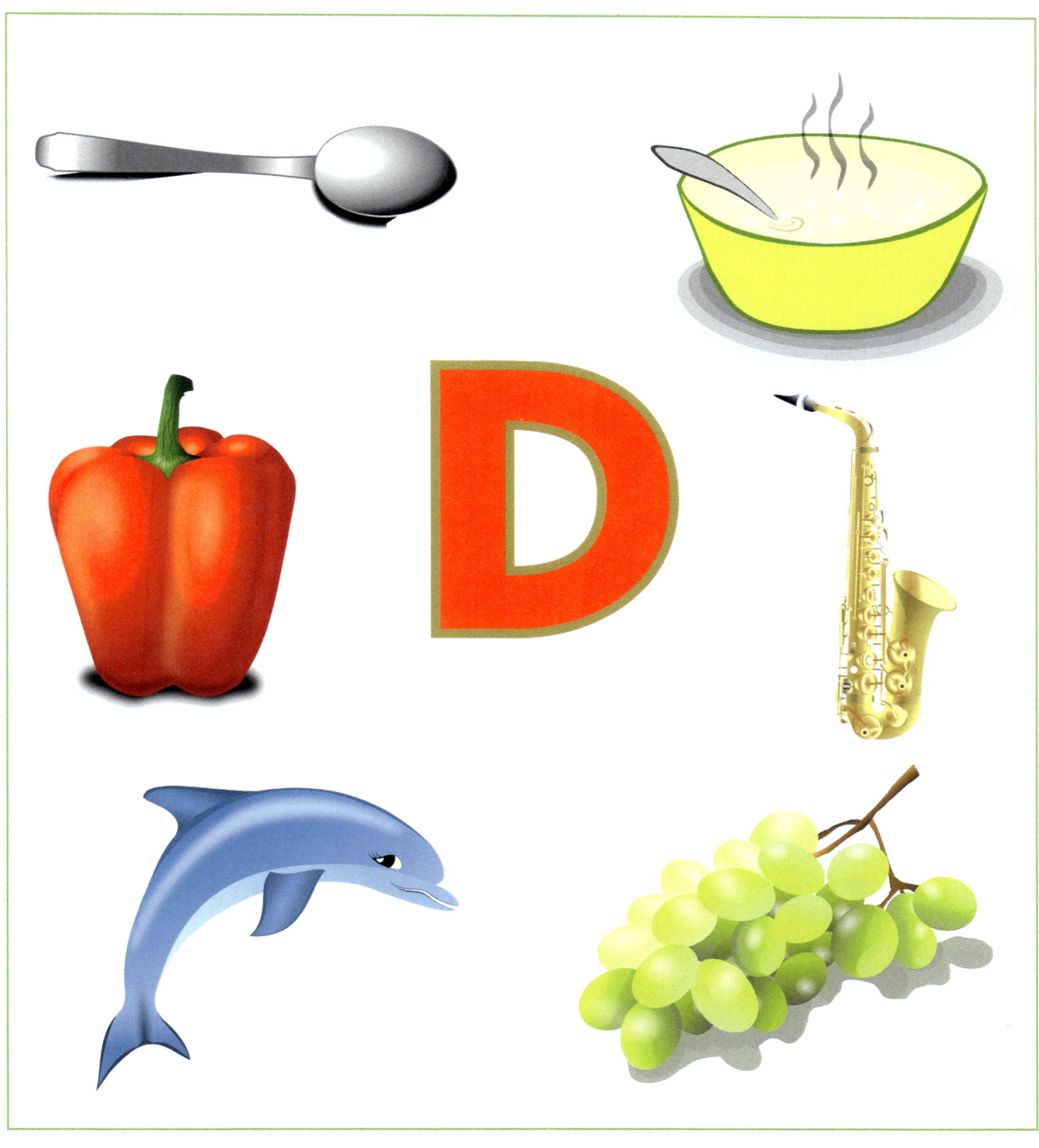

 **IS FOR**

DOLPHIN

I SPY with my smart eye, Something beginning with...

 IS FOR

ELEPHANT

I SPY with my smart eye, Something beginning with...

IS FOR

FISH

I SPY with my smart eye, Something beginning with...

G IS FOR

GRAPES

I SPY with my smart eye, Something beginning with...

IS FOR

HAMBERGER

I SPY with my smart eye,
Something beginning with...

IS FOR

ICE CREAM

I SPY with my smart eye, Something beginning with...

IS FOR

JUICE

I SPY with my smart eye, Something beginning with...

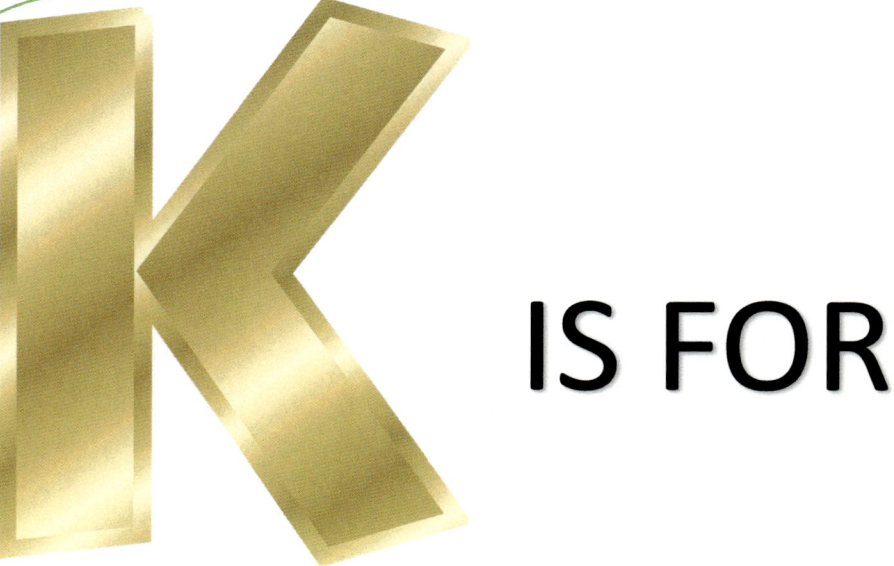 IS FOR

KIWI

I SPY with my smart eye, Something beginning with...

 IS FOR

LIGHT

I SPY with my smart eye, Something beginning with...

M IS FOR

MANGO

I SPY with my smart eye, Something beginning with...

 IS FOR

NECTARINE

I SPY with my smart eye, Something beginning with...

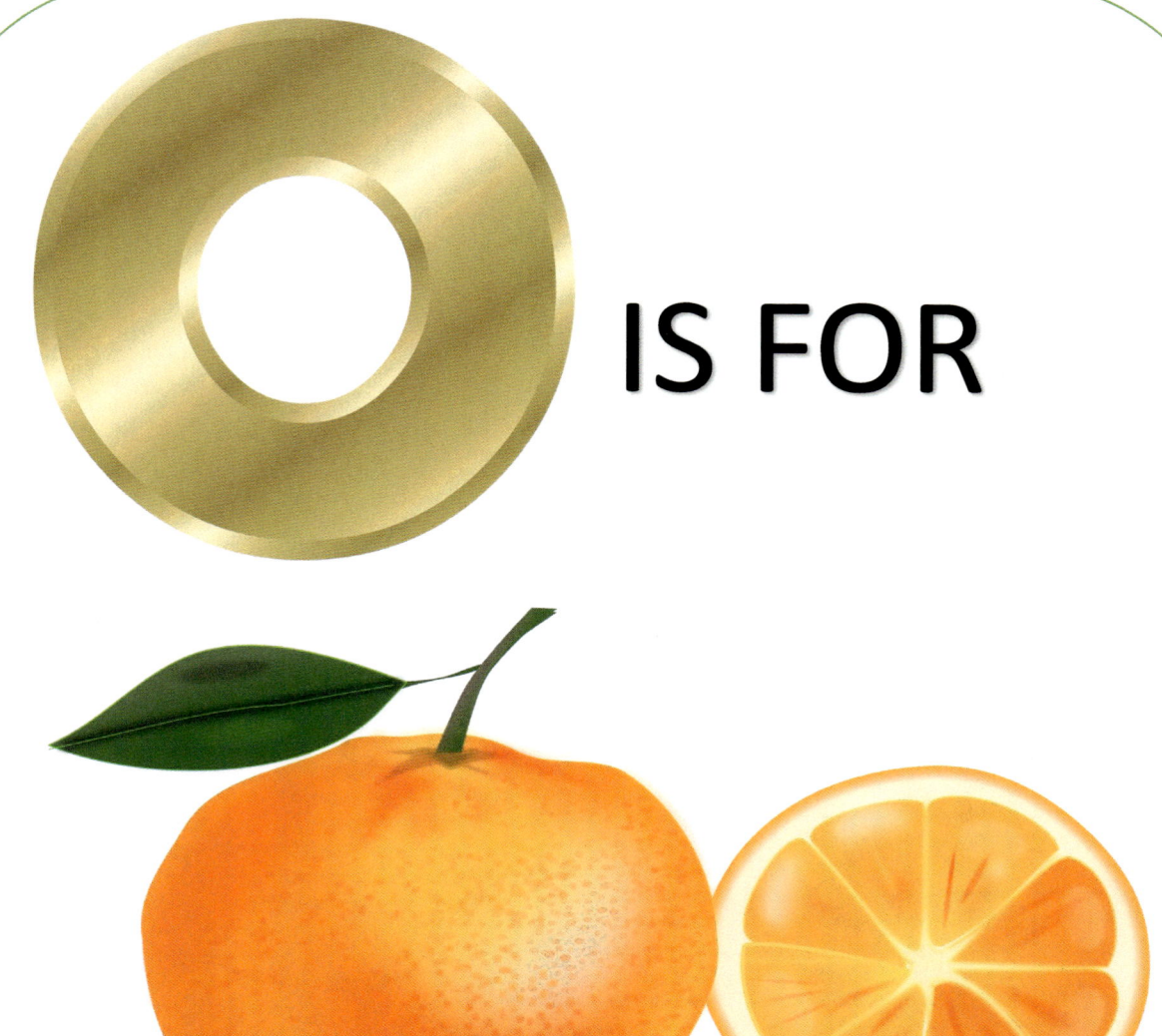

IS FOR

ORANGE

I SPY with my smart eye, Something beginning with...

 IS FOR

PAPAYA

I SPY with my smart eye, Something beginning with...

 IS FOR

QUAIL

I SPY with my smart eye, Something beginning with...

 IS FOR

Rooster

I SPY with my smart eye, Something beginning with...

 IS FOR

Strawberry

I SPY with my smart eye, Something beginning with...

T IS FOR

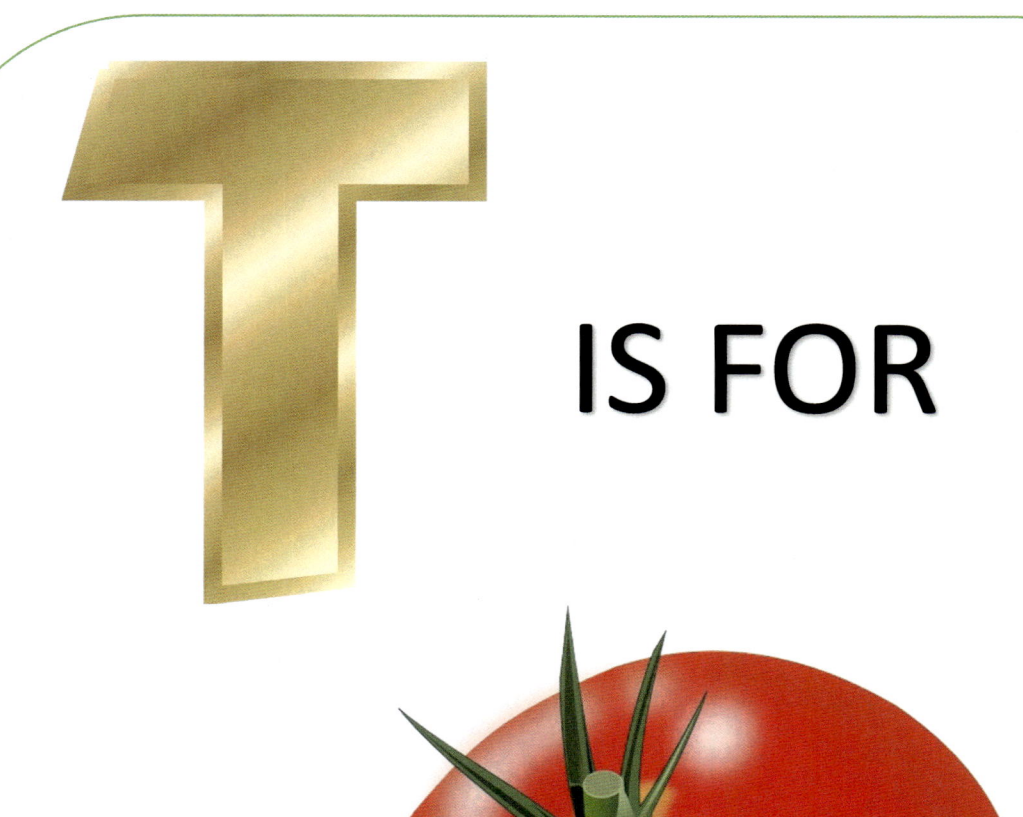

Tomato

I SPY with my smart eye, Something beginning with...

U IS FOR

Umbrella

I SPY with my smart eye, Something beginning with...

V IS FOR

Violin

I SPY with my smart eye, Something beginning with...

 IS FOR

WHALE

I SPY with my smart eye, Something beginning with...

 IS FOR

XYLOPHONE

I SPY with my smart eye, Something beginning with...

 IS FOR

YOLK

I SPY with my smart eye, Something beginning with...

 IS FOR

ZEBRA

Made in the USA
Middletown, DE
12 November 2020